super cute
WORLD

A Coloring &
Creativity Book

This book colored by:

_____

Jane
Maday

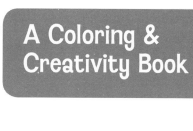

NORTH LIGHT BOOKS

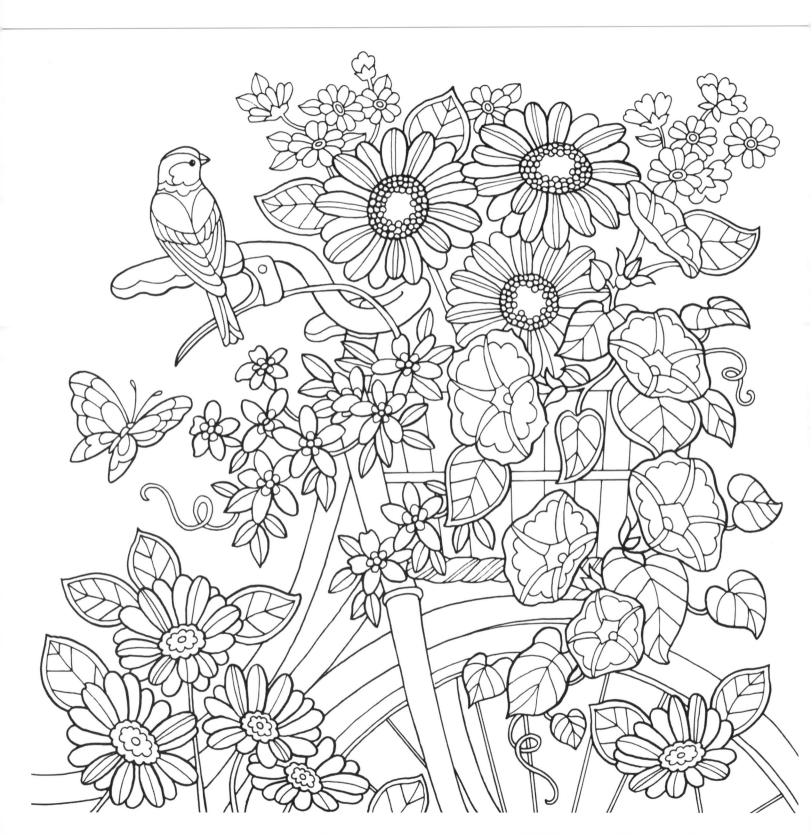

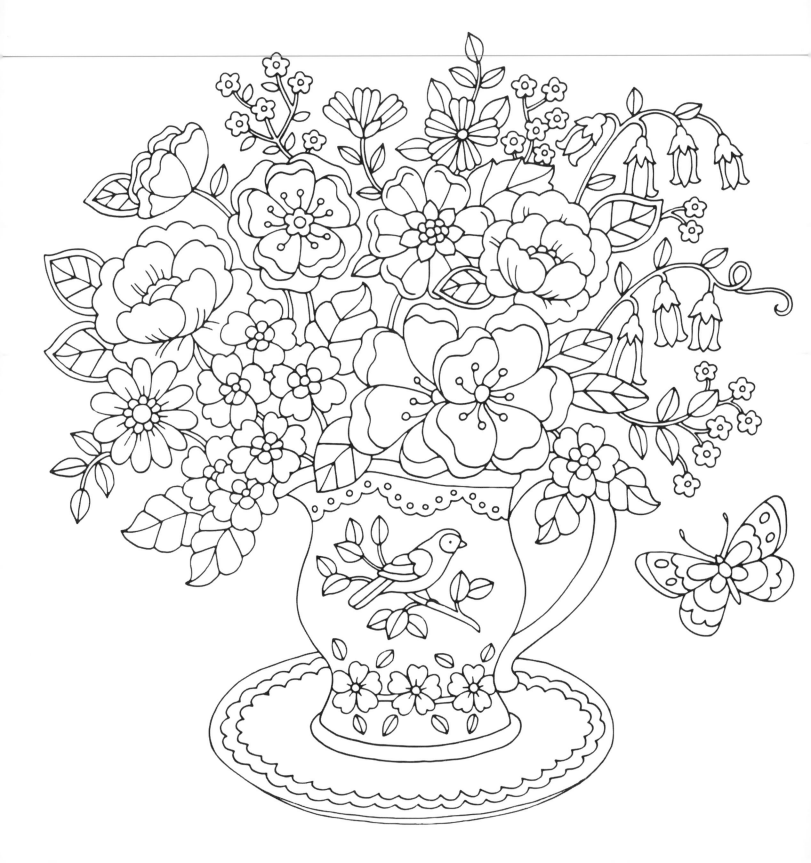

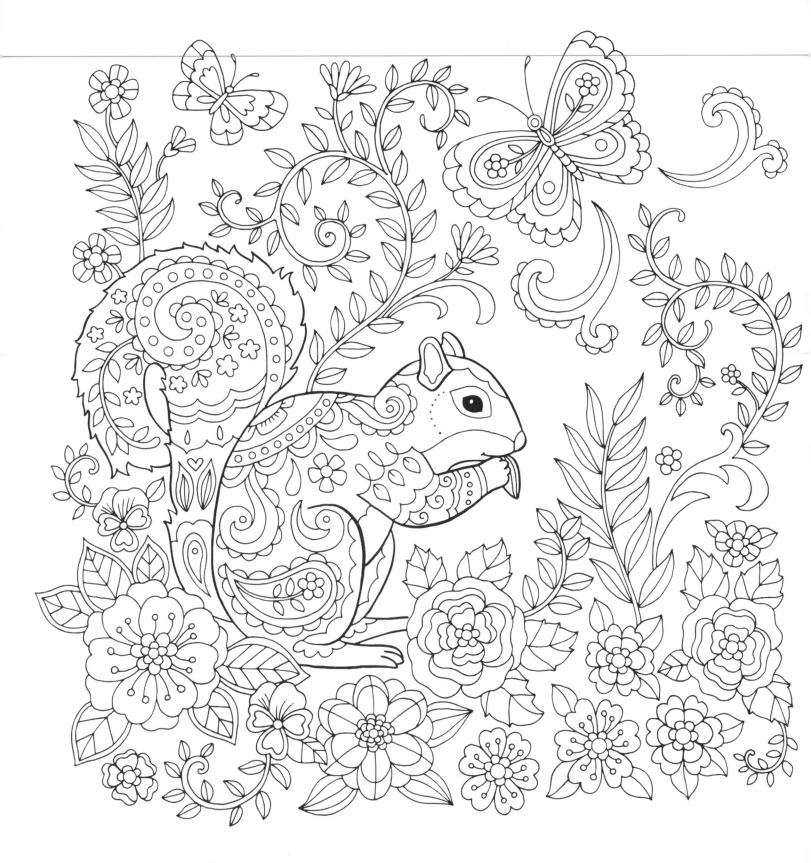

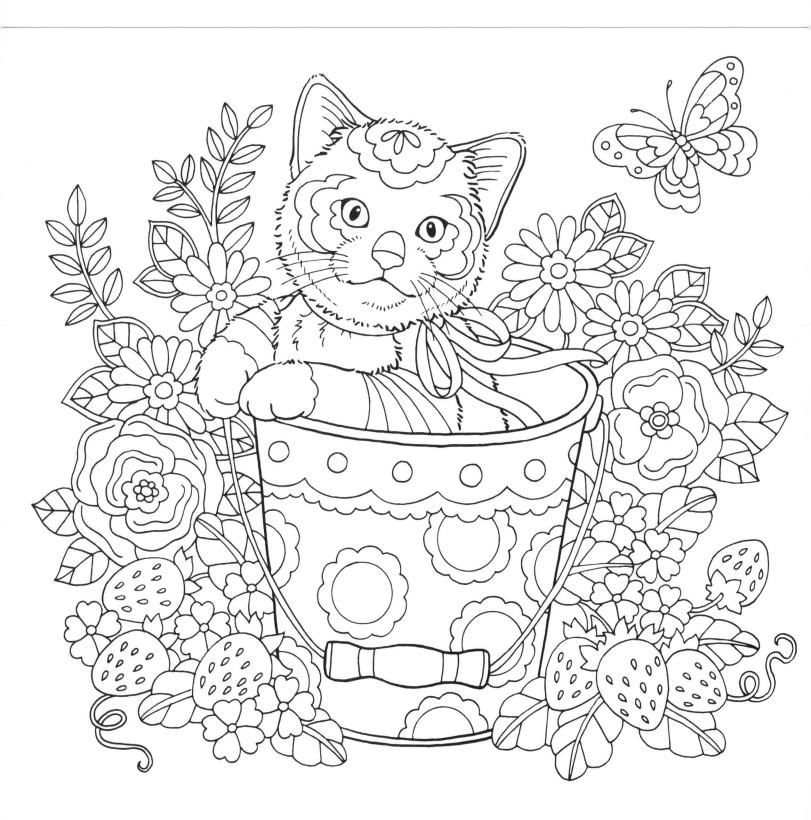

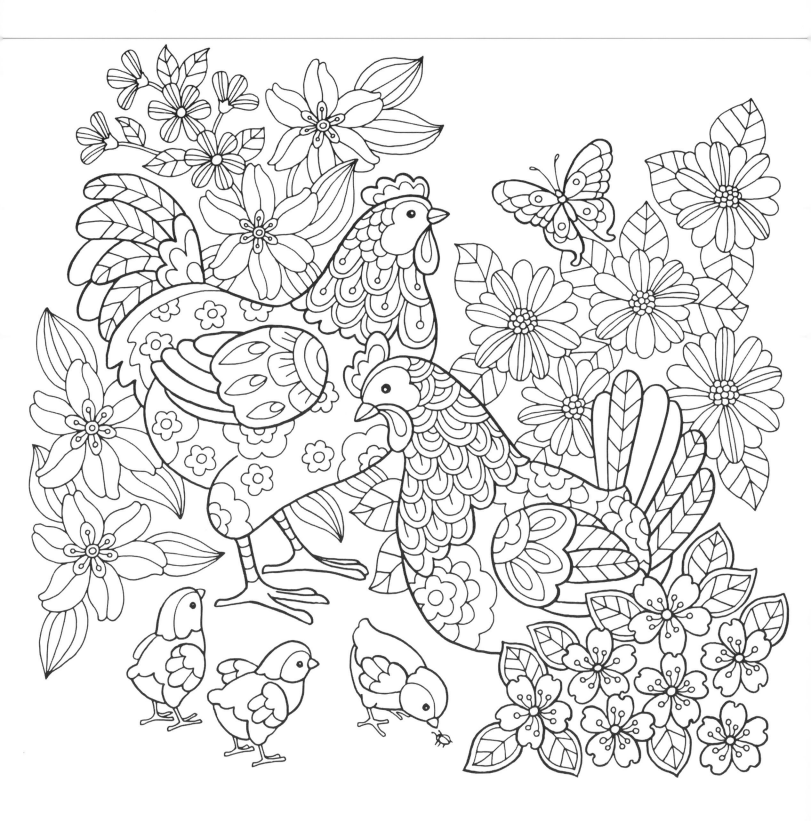

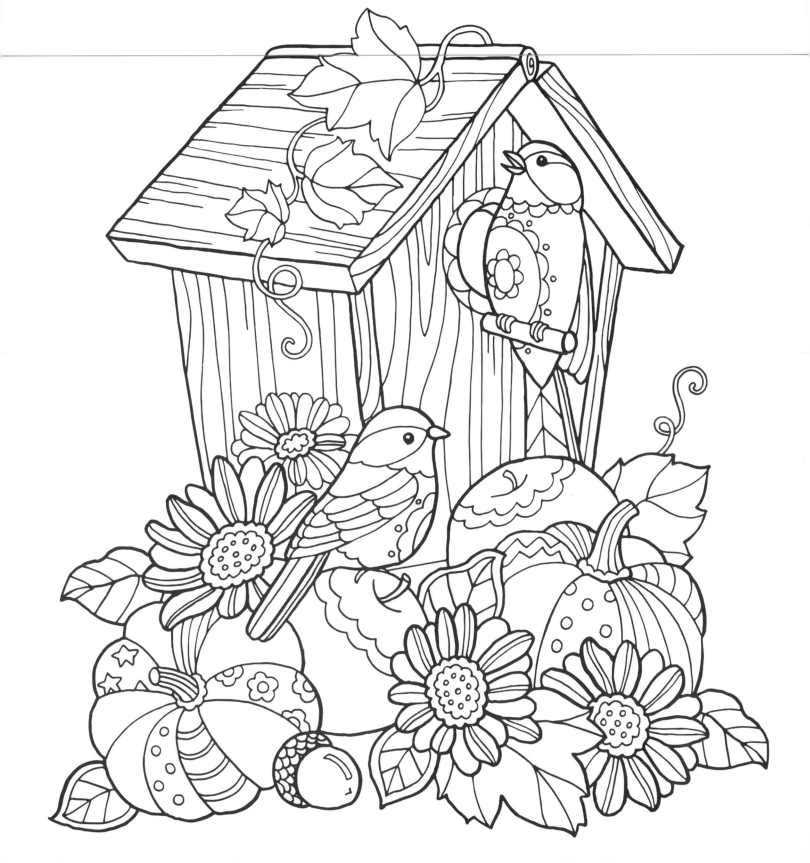

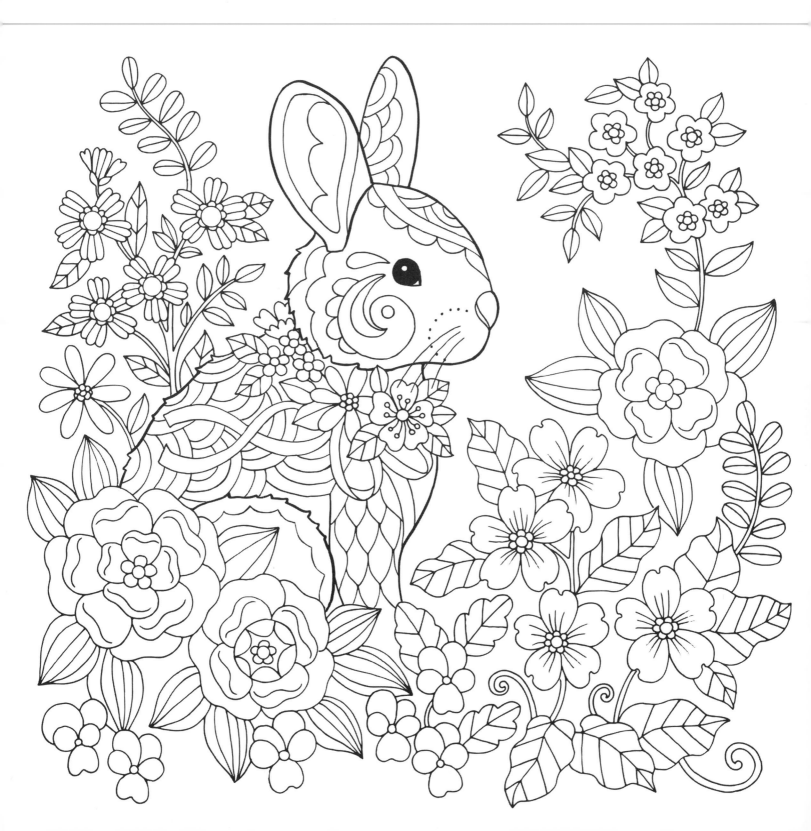

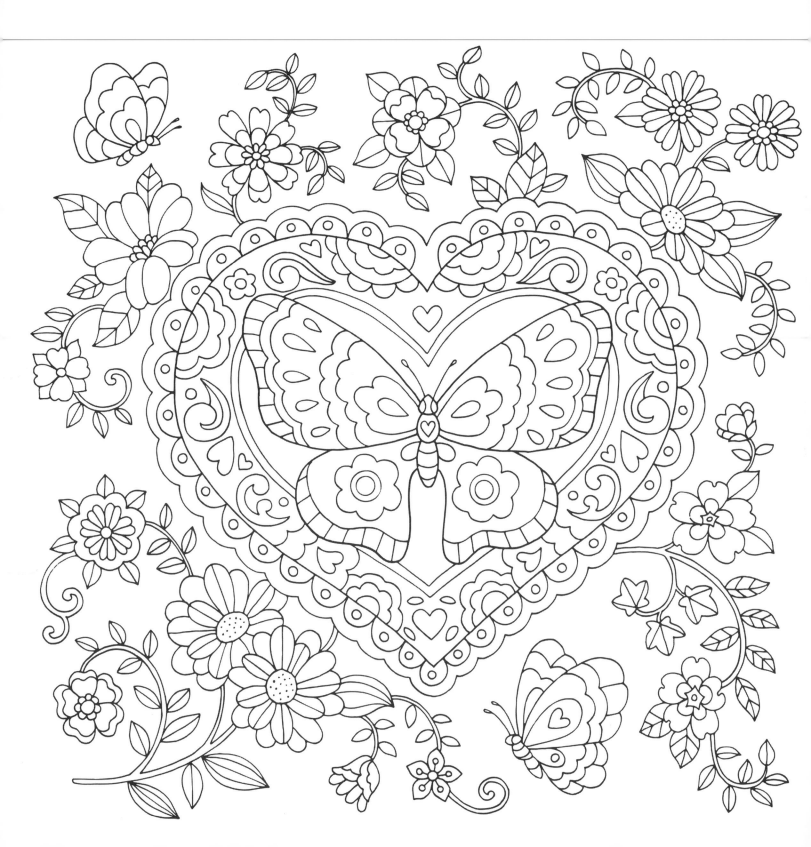

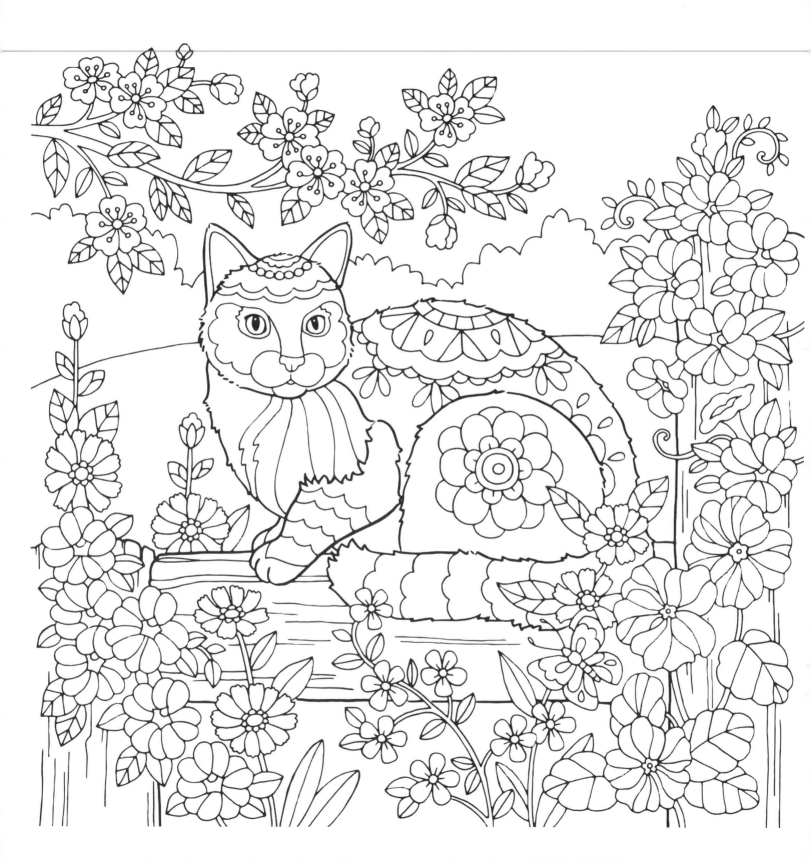

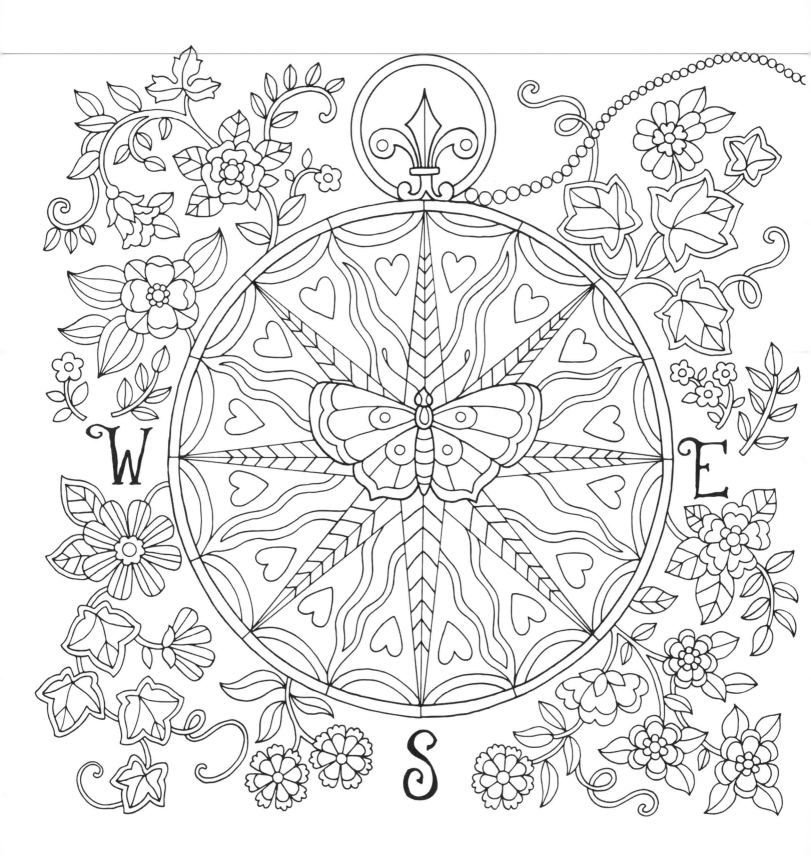

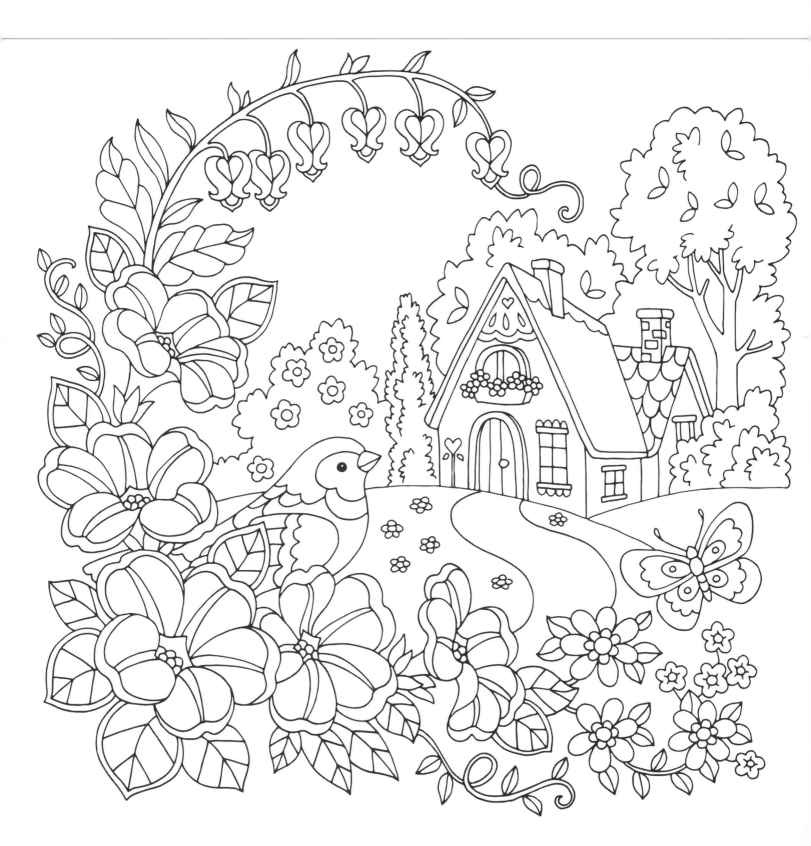

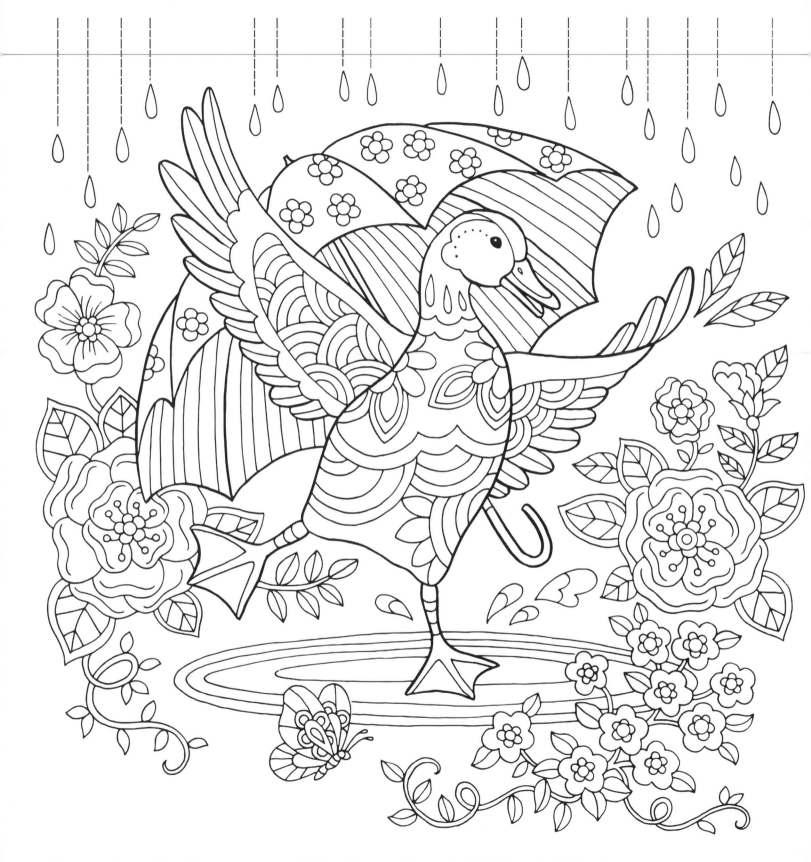

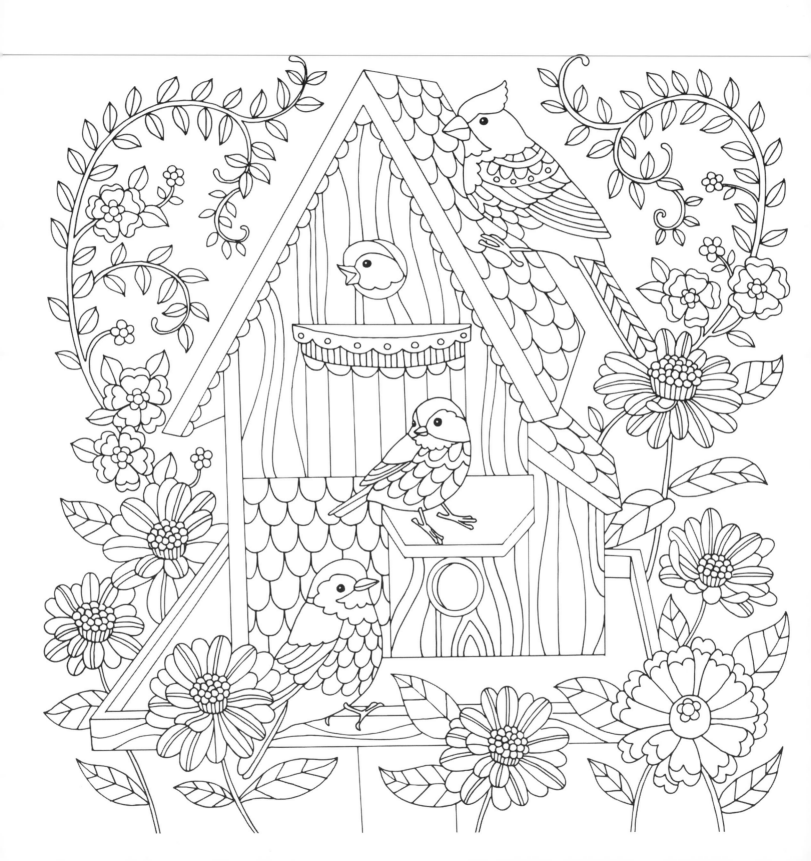

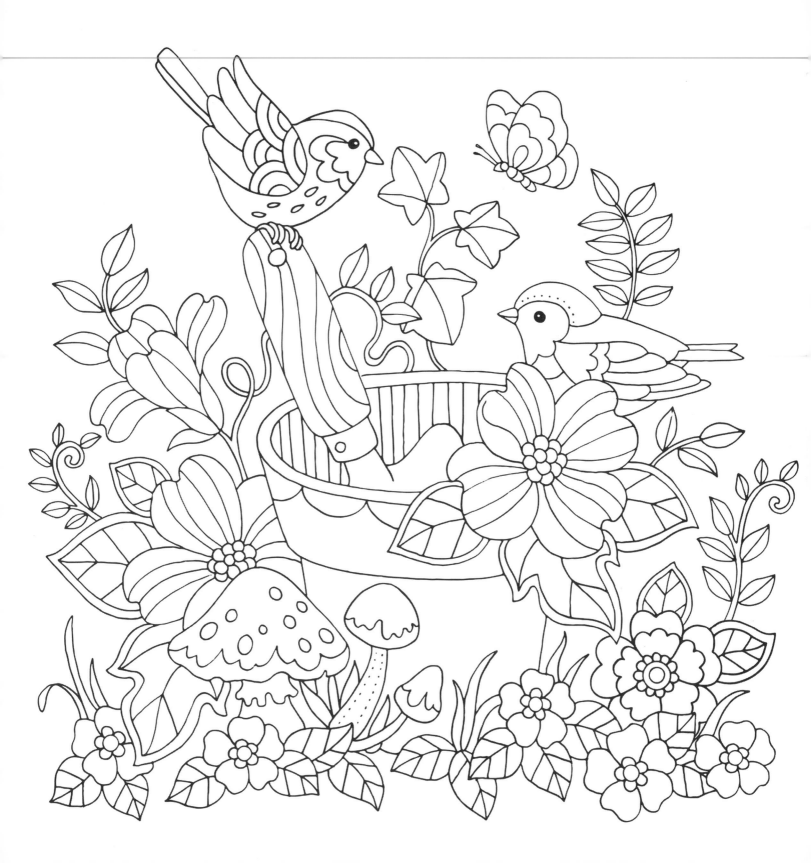

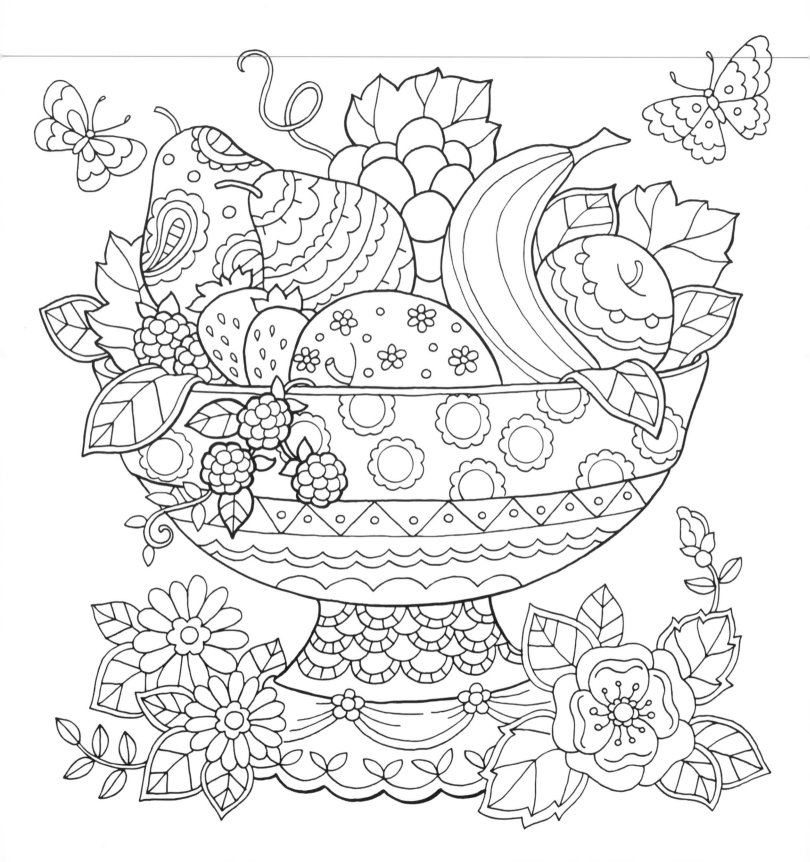

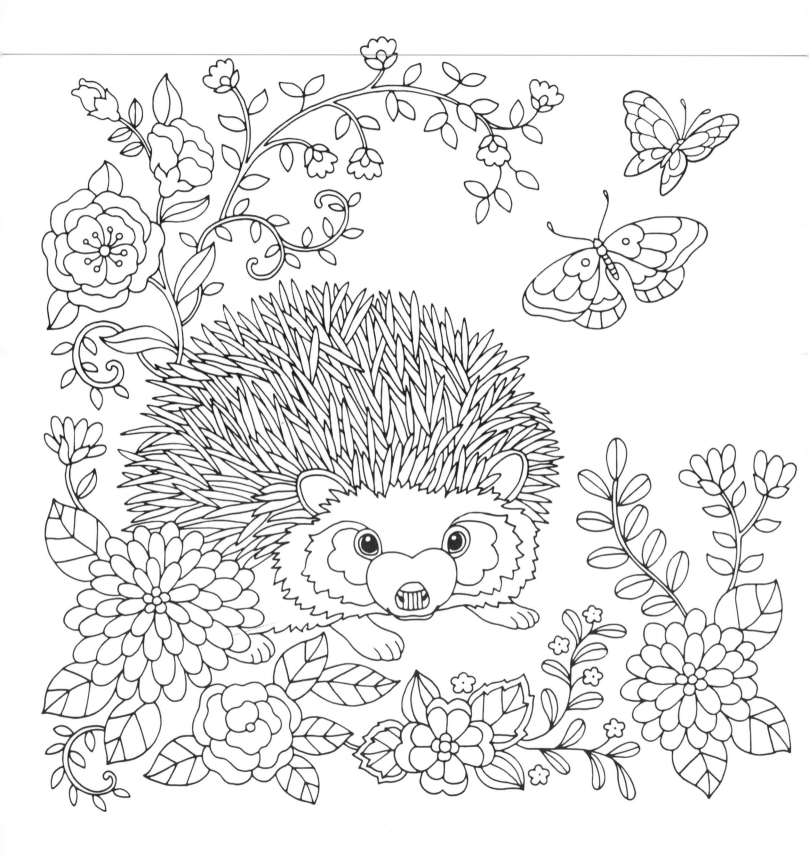

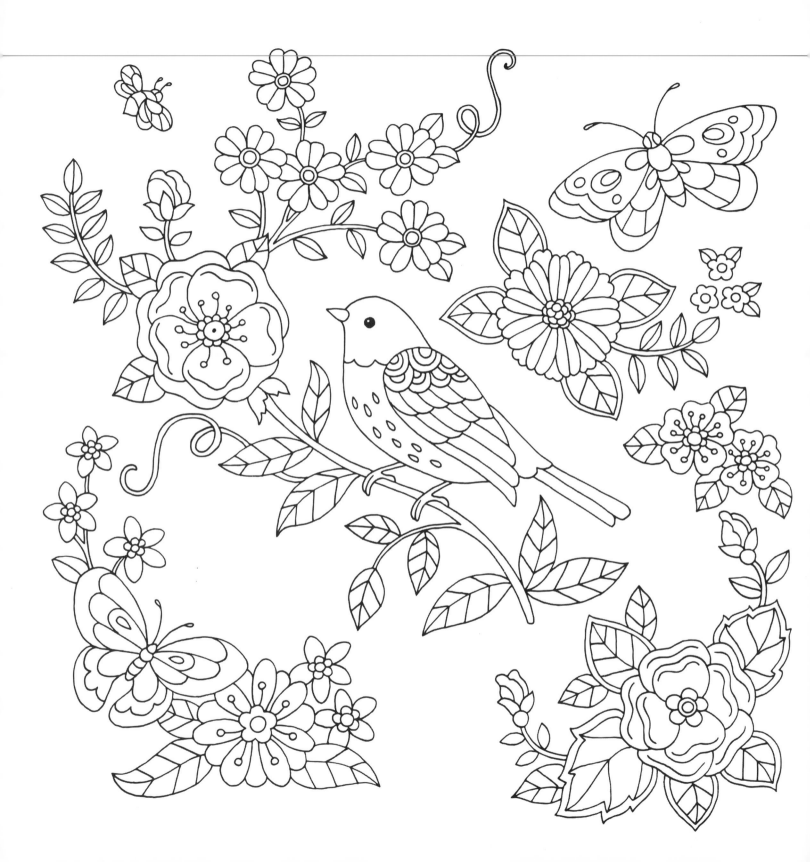

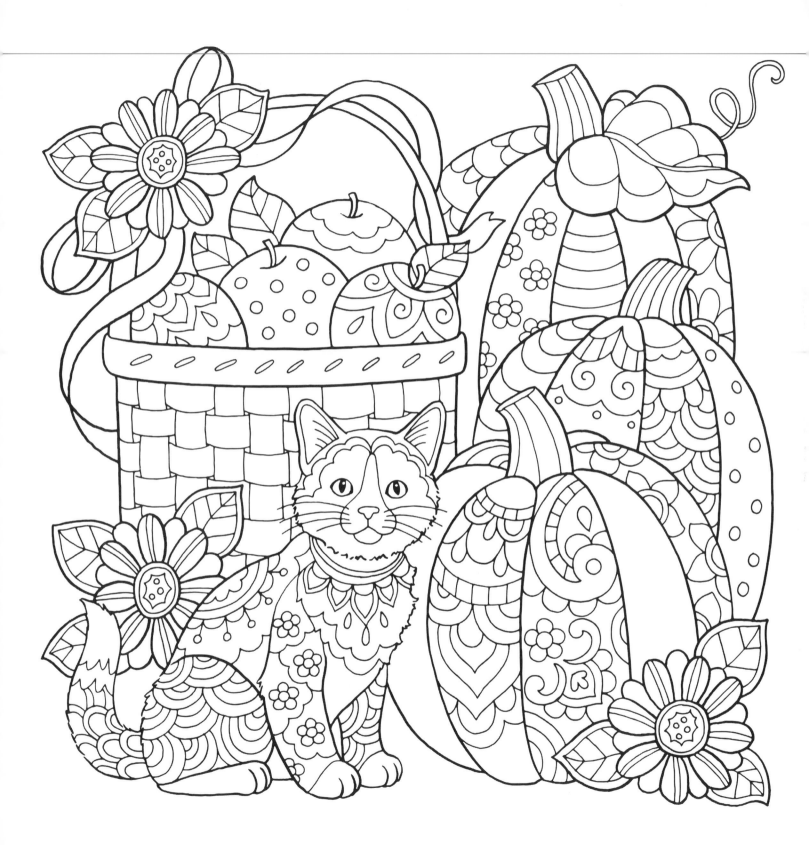

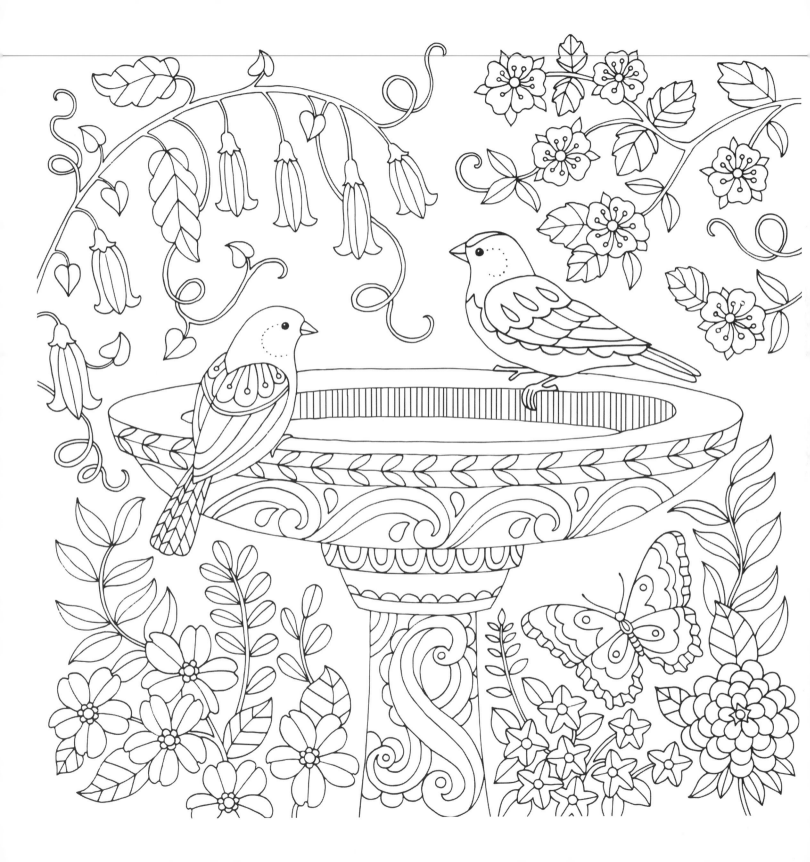

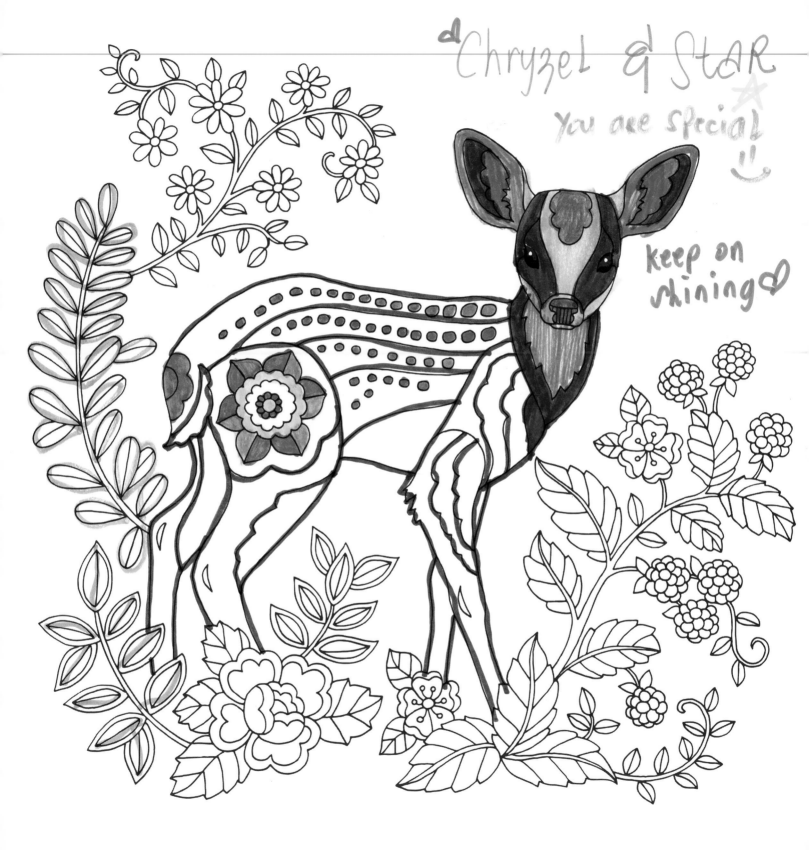

Chryzel & STAR

You are special !!

keep on shining

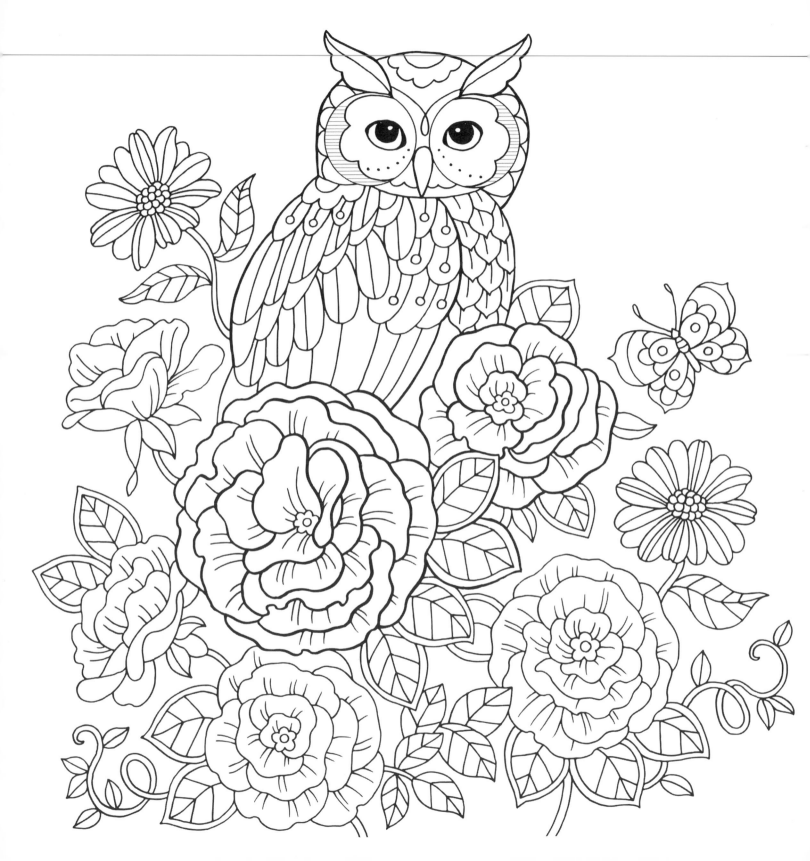

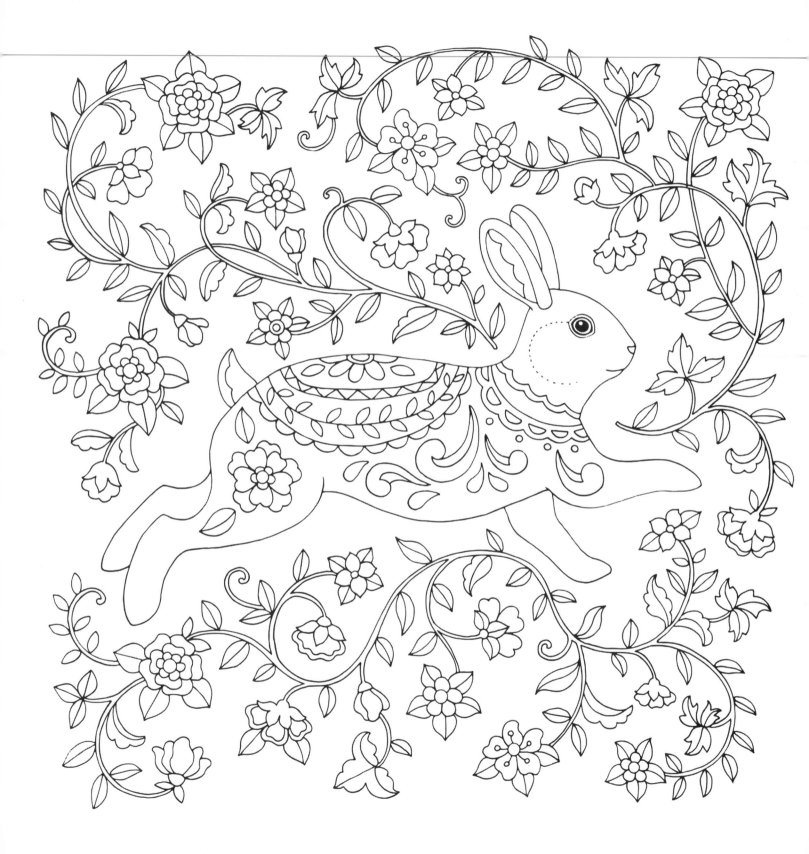

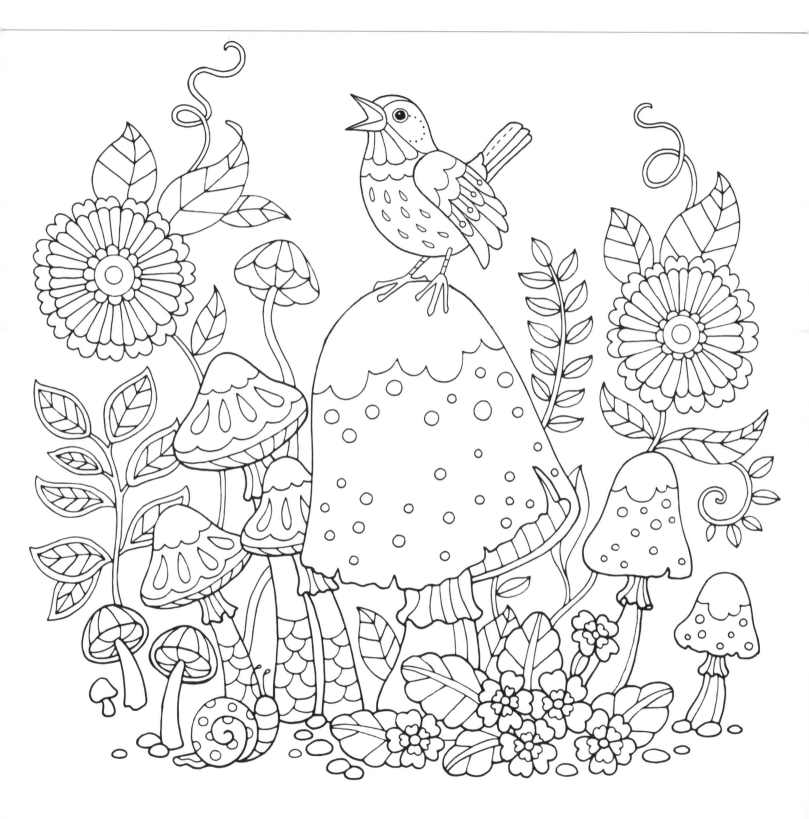

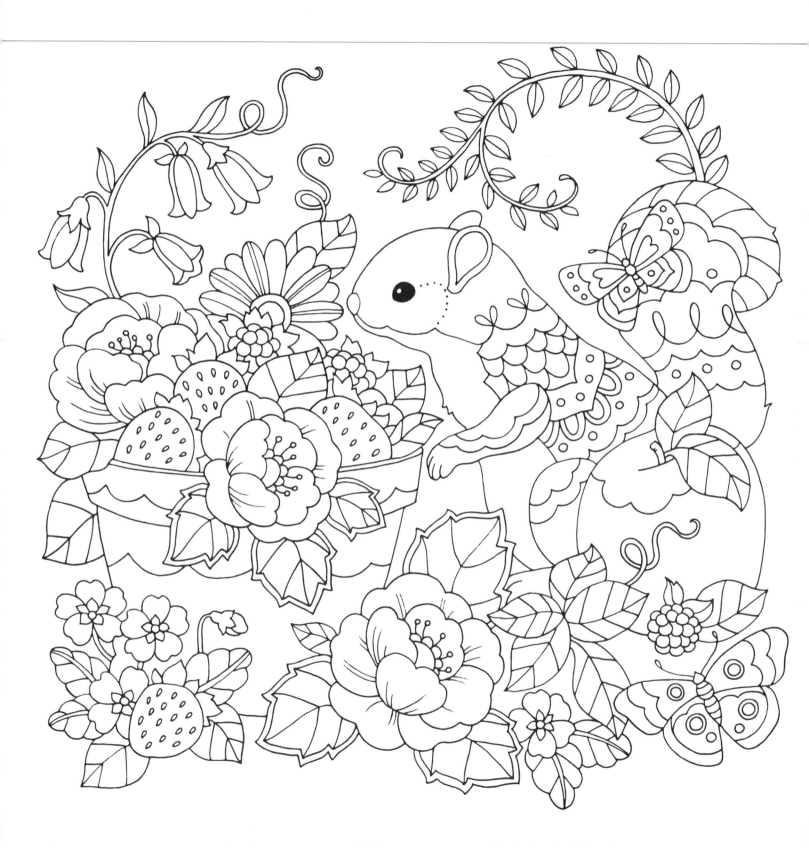

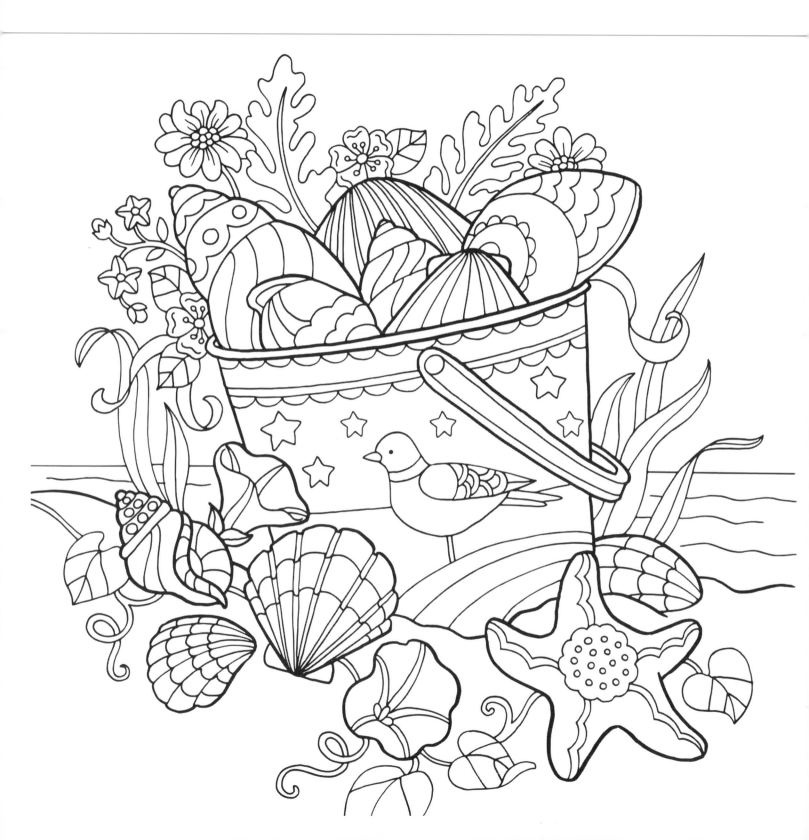

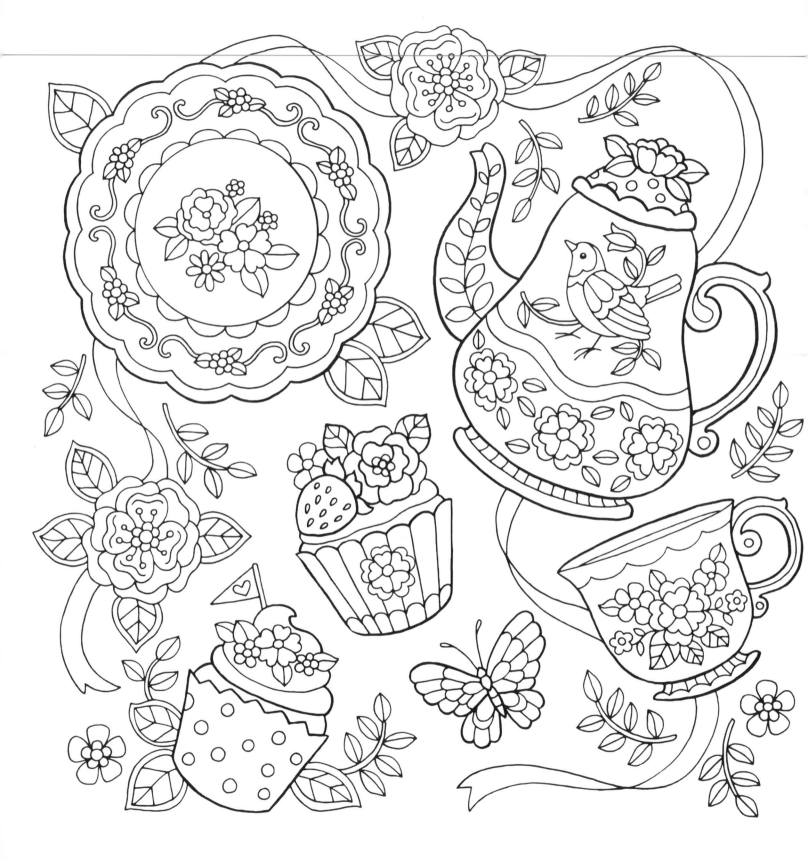

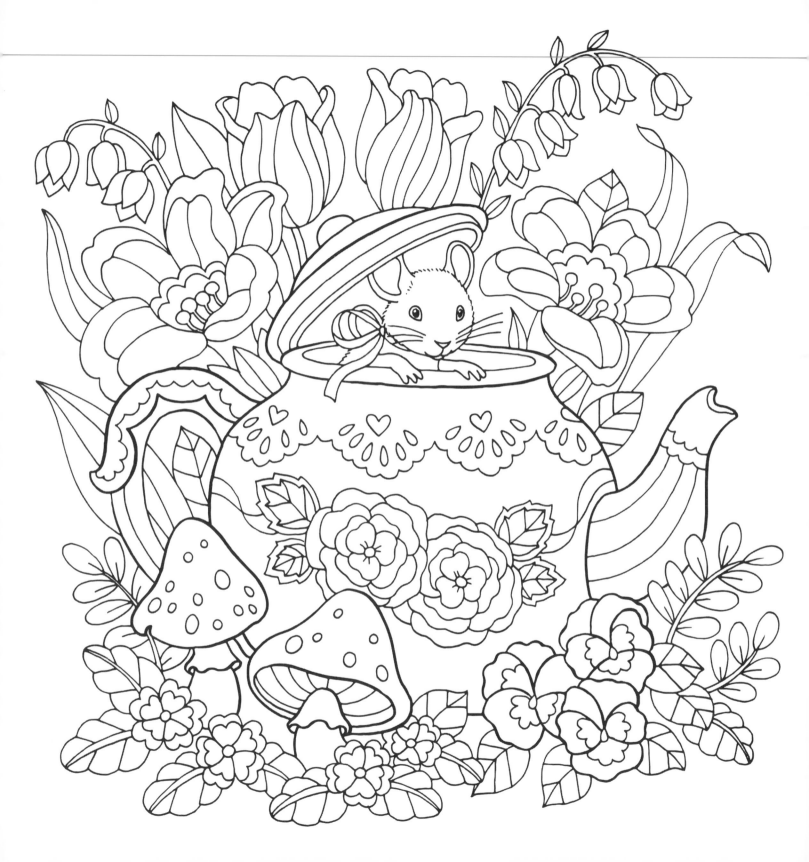

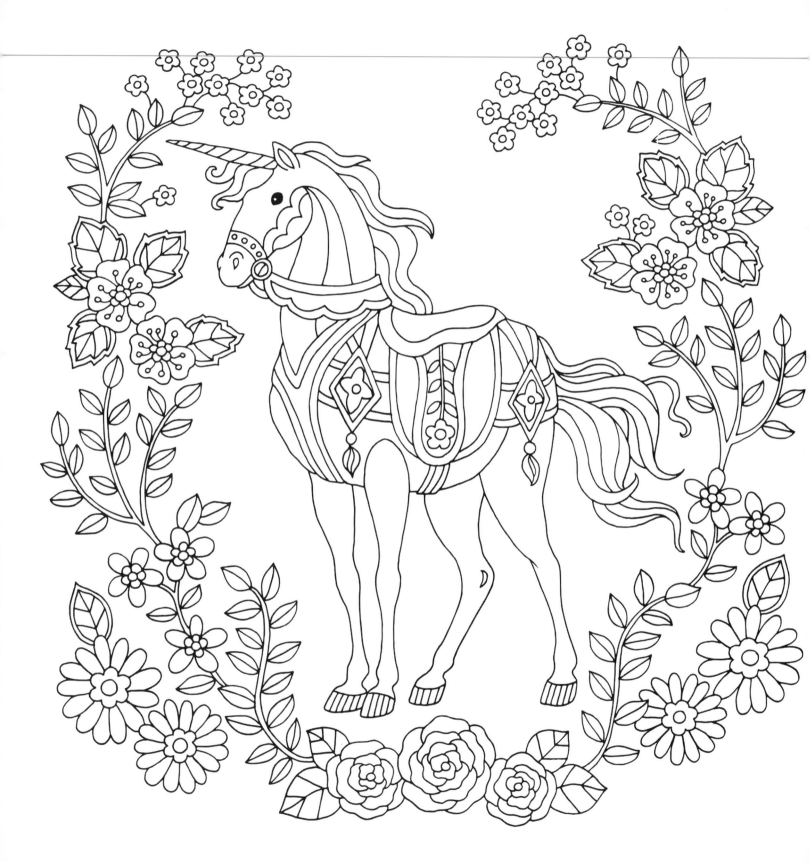

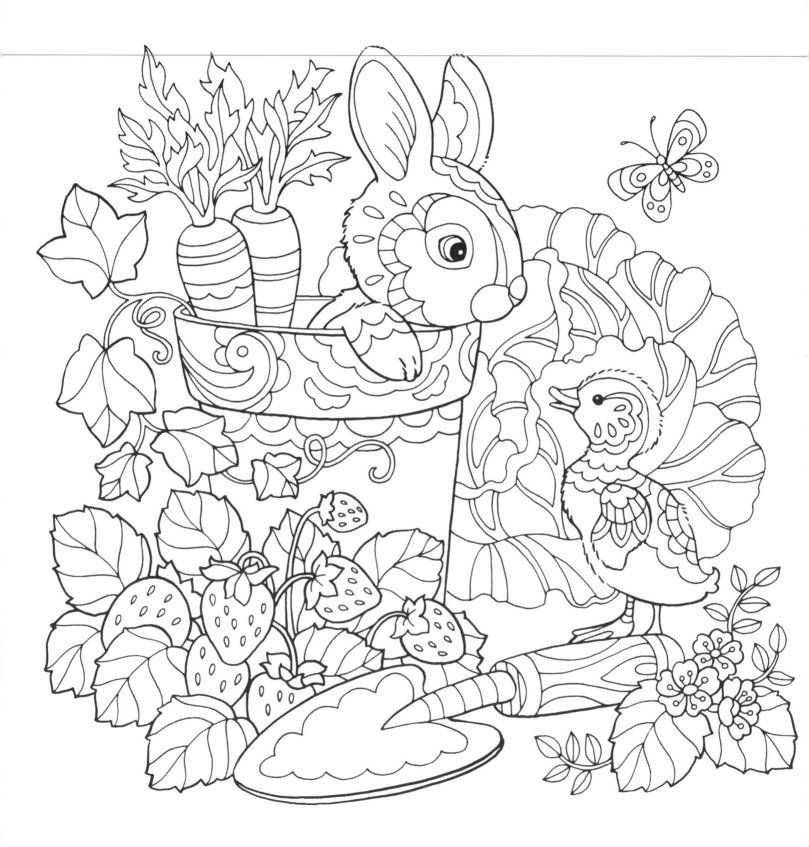

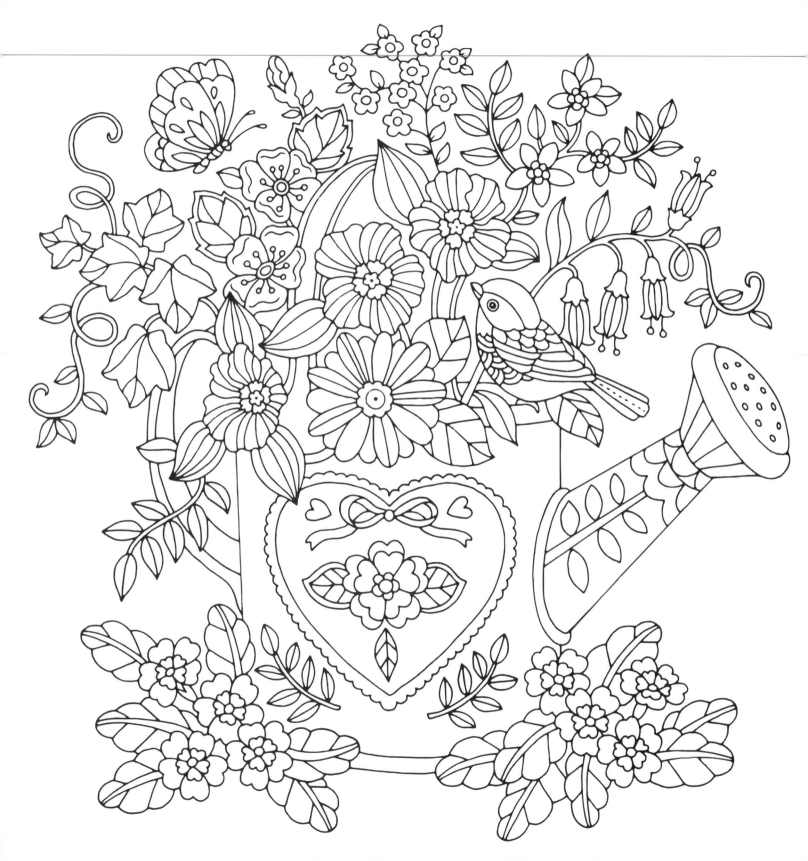

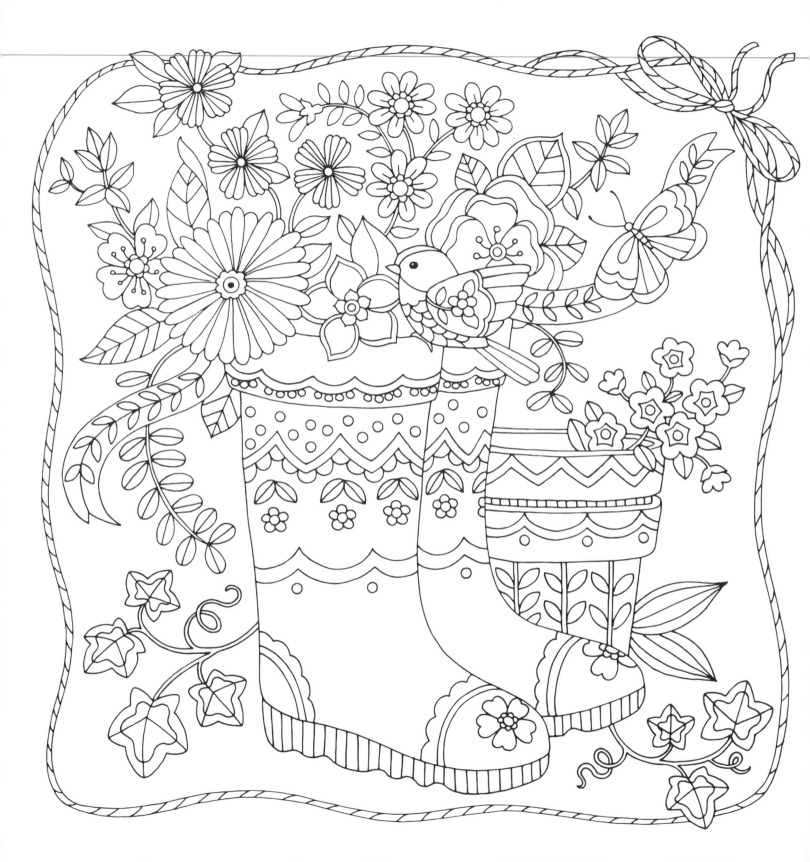

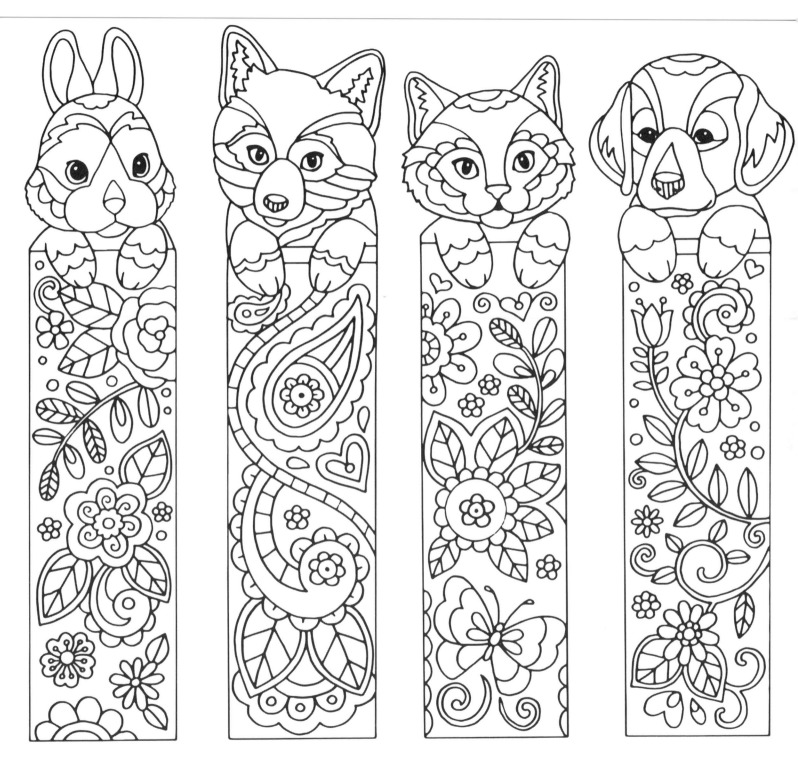

Here are some cute bookmarks to color and cut out. You may want to laminate them for extra sturdiness.

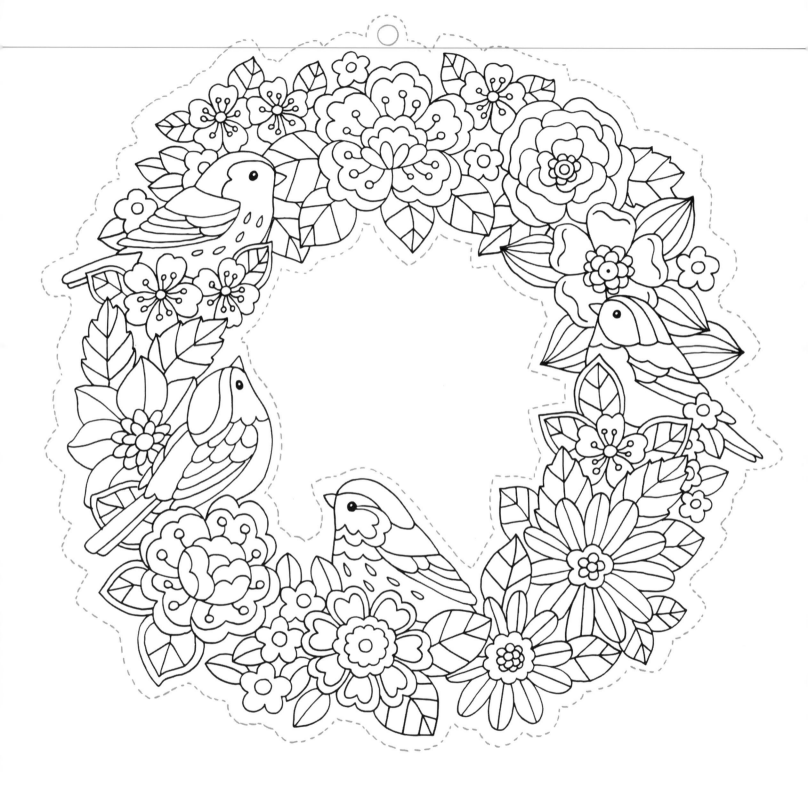

Color and cut out the wreath. Use thread or fishing line to hang it in the window.

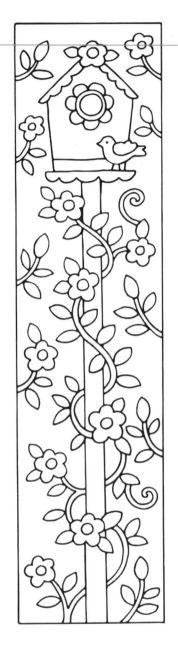
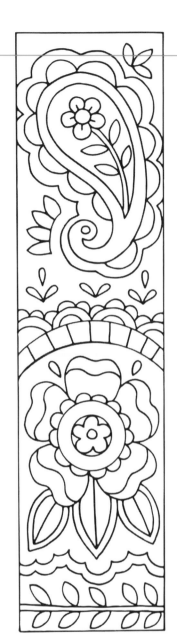
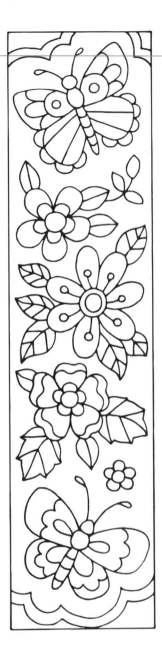
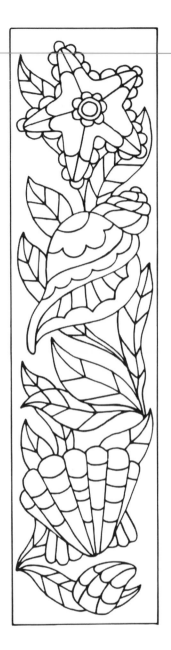
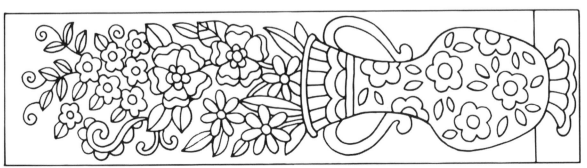

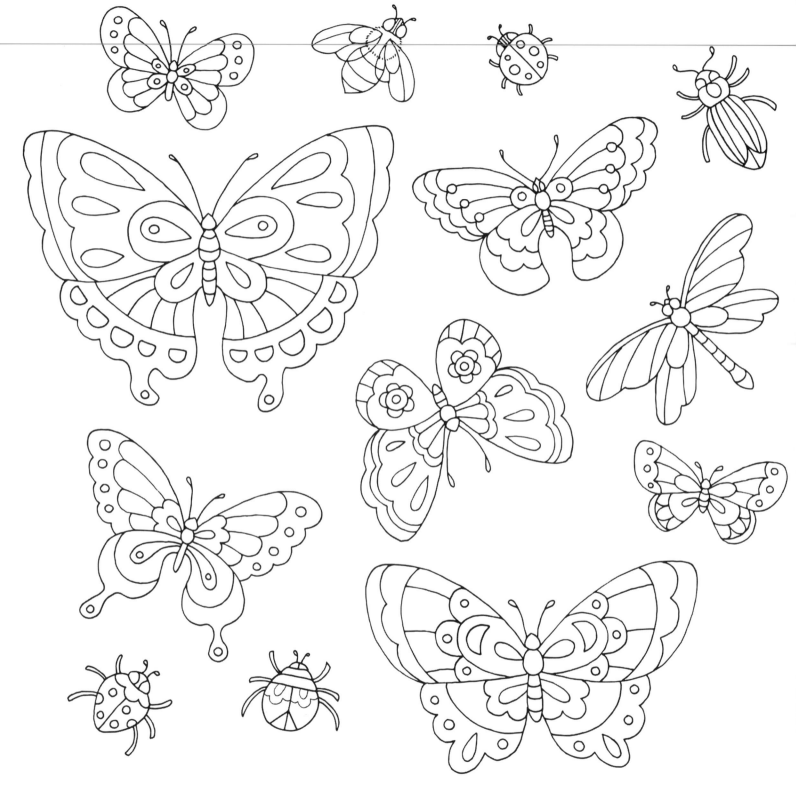

Use these bugs and butterflies for cardmaking and crafts.

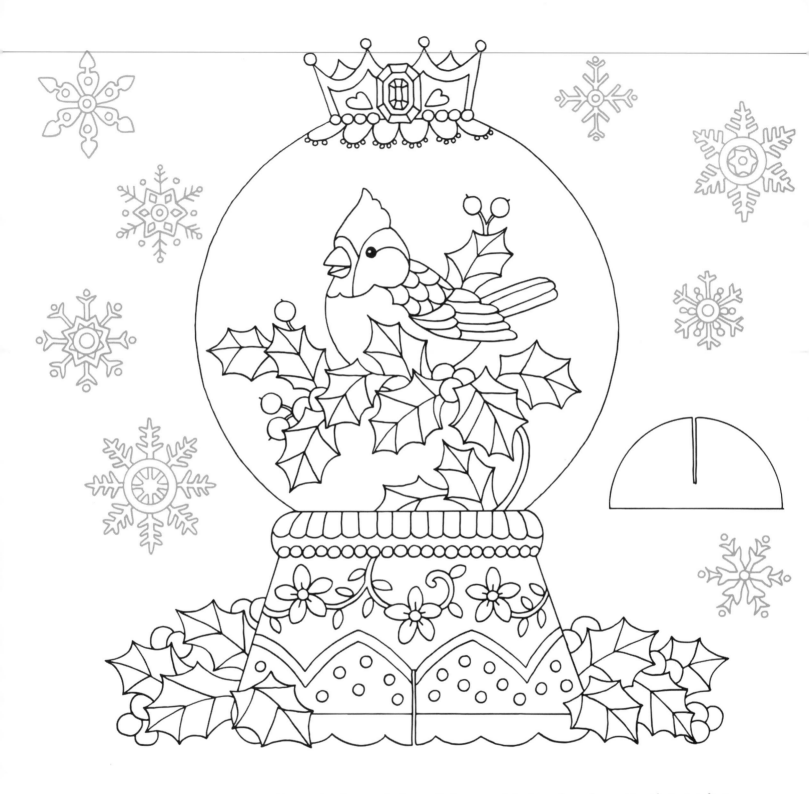

Color and cut out. Insert the stand into the slot on the base of the snowglobe to make a decoration that stands up.
Try adding glitter to increase the snowglobe effect.

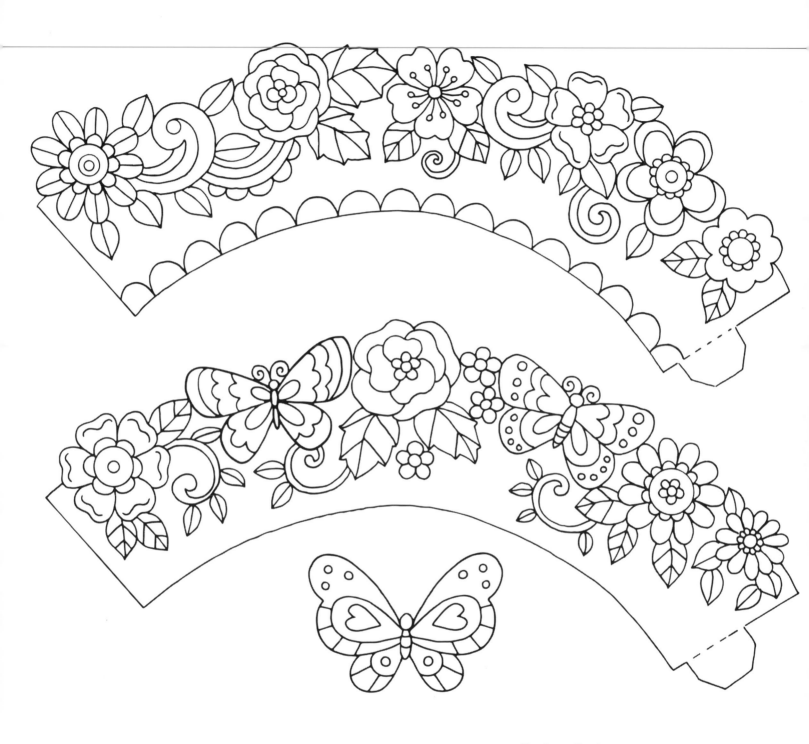

Copy and color these cupcake wrappers as many times as you like for a festive party.
Wrap them around the cupcake and glue with the tab.
You can overlap the edges to make them fit depending on the size of your cake.
Cut out the big butterfly and attach it to a toothpick to decorate the top of your cupcake.

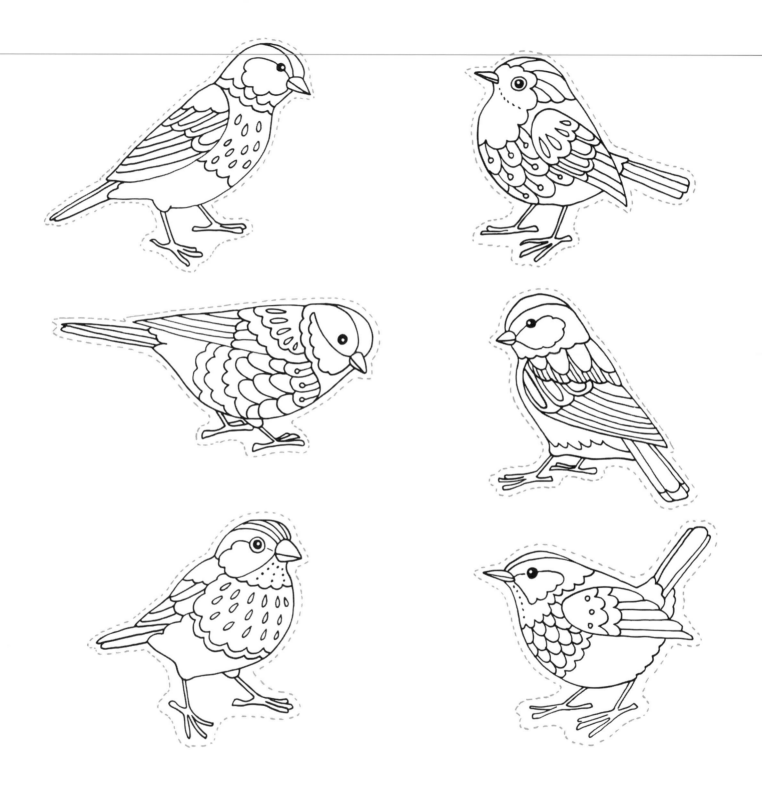

Use these cute birds for fun cardmaking and crafting.

Cut these garden images out and use them for crafting and scrapbooking.

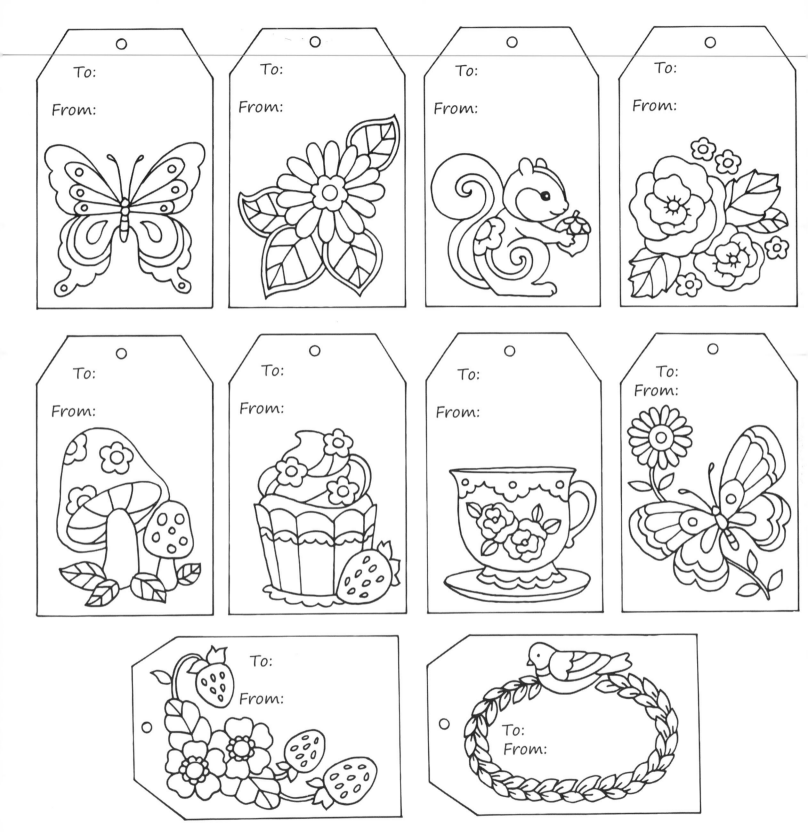

To:
From:

To:
From:

To:
From:

To:
From:

To:
From:

To:
From:

To:
From:

To:
From:

To:
From:

To:
From:

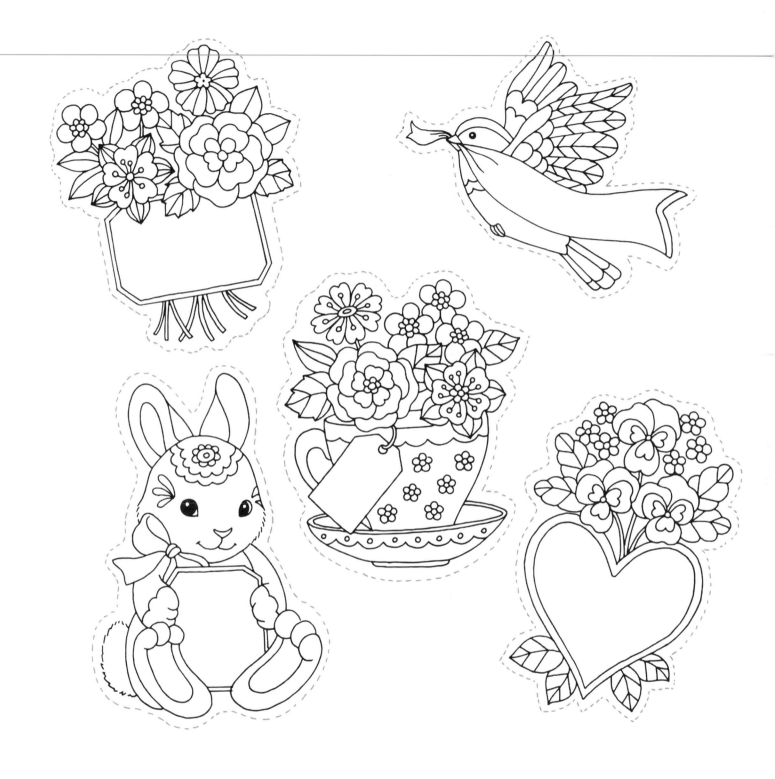

Use these as gift tags or print them on sticker paper to make labels.

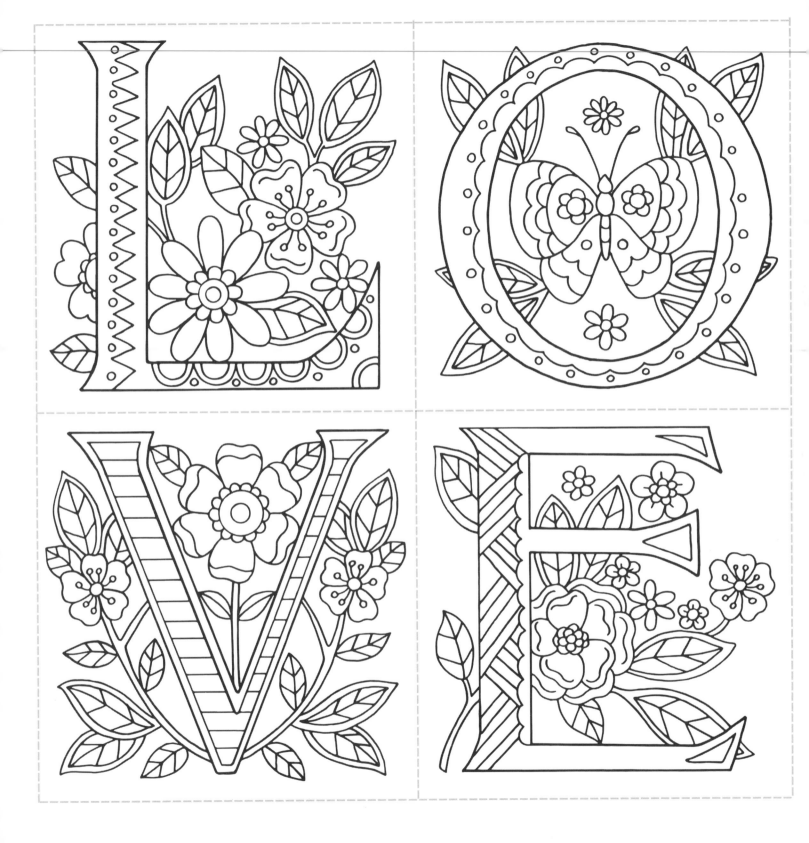

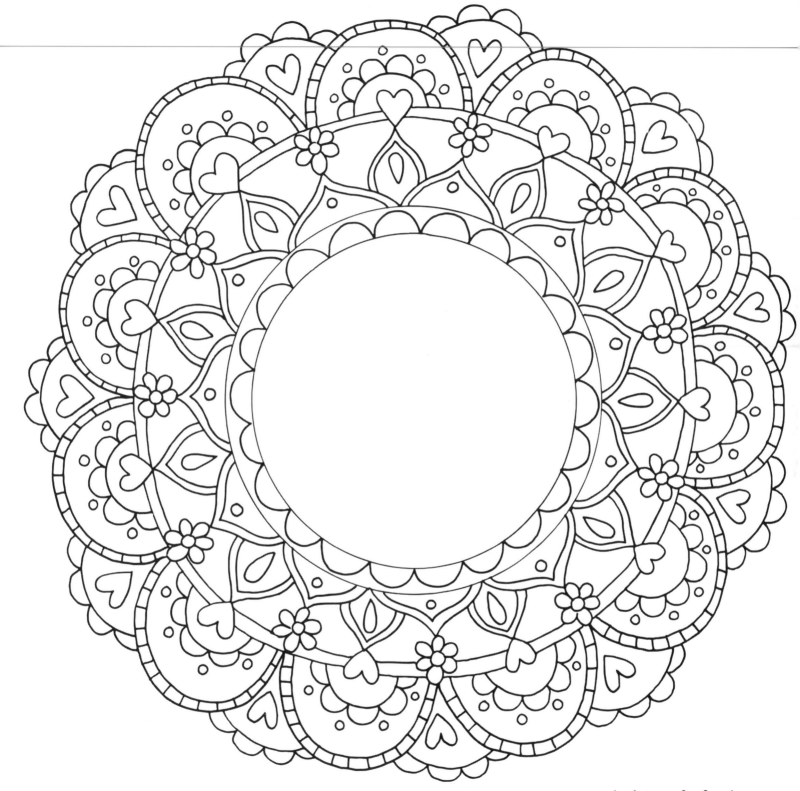

Write your favorite inspirational quote inside the mandala. Cut it out and mount it on pretty scrapbook paper for framing.

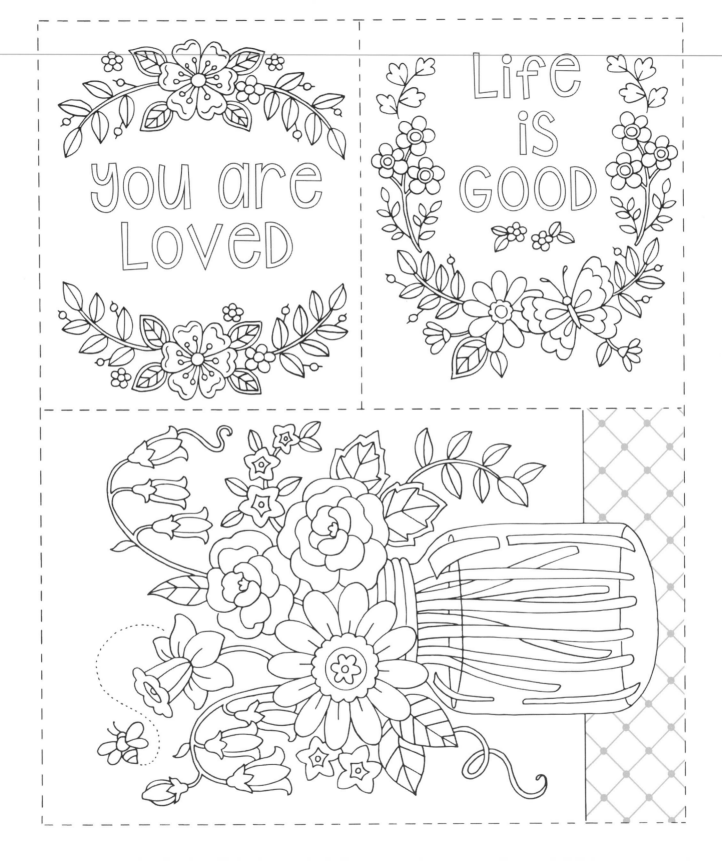

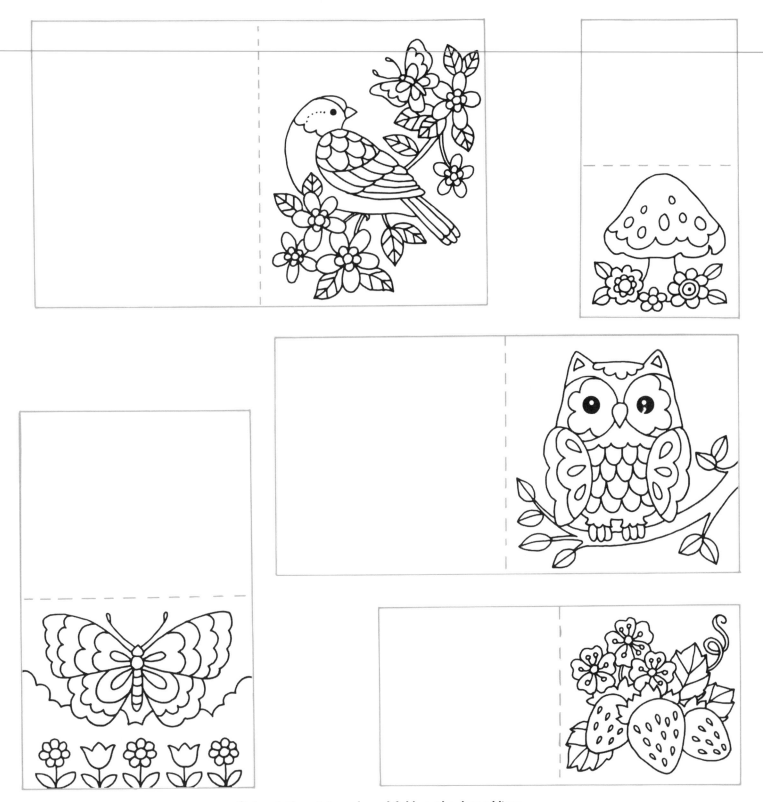

Cut out the mini cards and fold on the dotted lines.

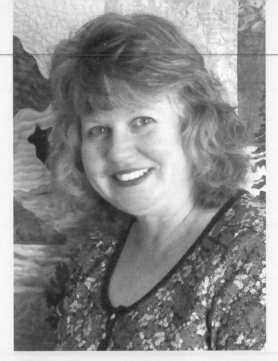

North Light Books
An imprint of Penguin Random House LLC
penguinrandomhouse.com

Printed in Mexico
10th Printing

ISBN 978-1-4403-4975-1

Edited by Beth Erikson
Designed by Geoffrey Raker

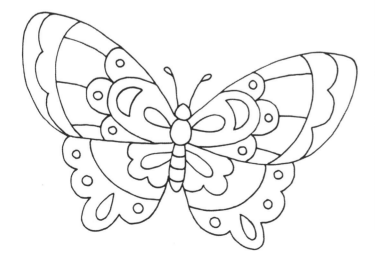

About the Author

Born in England and raised in the
United States, Jane Maday has been a
professional artist since she was 14 years
old. At 16, she was hired by the University
of Florida as a scientific illustrator. After
graduating from the Ringling College of
Art and Design, Jane was recruited by
Hallmark Cards, Inc., as a greeting card
illustrator. She left the corporate world
after her children were born and now
licenses her work for products such as
cards, flags, puzzles, gifts and home
decor. Jane lives in scenic Colorado with
her husband and children. This is her fifth
book for North Light. Visit her website at
janemaday.com.

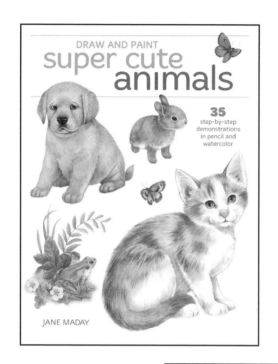
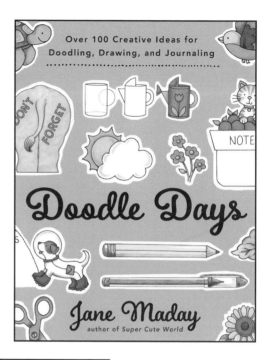
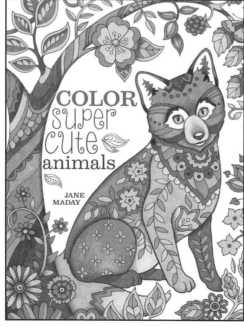